BIKING COUNTRY

YORKSHIRE DALES
CYCLE WAY

Richard Peace

Illustrated by
Paul Hannon

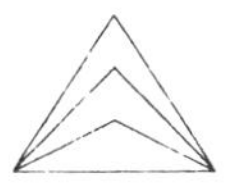

HILLSIDE

RICHARD PEACE is a freelance teacher and writer. He was educated at Queen Elizabeth Grammar School, Wakefield and Magdalen College, Oxford, obtaining a degree in Modern History.

He lives in Wakefield, West Yorkshire and when not cycling or walking in Britain he travels and teaches abroad.

At Embsay

BY THE SAME AUTHOR

- YORKSHIRE DALES CYCLE WAY
- WEST YORKSHIRE CYCLE WAY
- MOUNTAIN BIKING - WEST & SOUTH YORKSHIRE
(all Hillside Guides)
- THE MACLEHOSE TRAIL (WALKING: HONG KONG)

A full list of current Hillside guides can be found at the end of the book

BIKING COUNTRY

YORKSHIRE DALES *CYCLE WAY*

Richard Peace

Illustrated by
Paul Hannon

HILLSIDE

**HILLSIDE
PUBLICATIONS**
11 Nessfield Grove
Keighley
West Yorkshire
BD22 6NU

First published 1994
2nd impression 1996

Text © Richard Peace 1994
Illustrations © Paul Hannon 1994

ISBN 1 870141 28 8

*Cover illustrations:
Front: At Malham Tarn
Back: Swaledale from Oxnop Head;
Bolton Castle; Barden Bridge
(Paul Hannon/Big Country Picture Library)*

Printed in Great Britain by
Carnmor Print and Design
95-97 London Road
Preston
Lancashire
PR1 4BA

CONTENTS

*The Sportsman's Inn
Cowgill, Dentdale*

INTRODUCTION

The Yorkshire Dales Cycle Way is a major cycling route encircling the Yorkshire Dales National Park. Approximately 130 miles (210 kilometres) in length, it was designated such by the National Park Authority in conjunction with the Cyclists' Touring Club, to encourage sensible recreational use and appreciation of the Dales.

A number of cycleways exist nationally: the roads are not specially marked, but the lengthy circular tours are designated cycleways as they avoid main and busy roads where possible, and pass through areas of beauty or historical interest. A nearby companion to the Yorkshire Dales Cycle Way is the West Yorkshire Cycle Route. A fit cyclist should easily complete the whole route in a week, but attempting it in this time is certainly not advisable to someone without at least some previous experience of cycling.

The route is waymarked periodically. A white cycle on a blue background with a white arrow indicates the correct route. Although ambitious, the Way takes in some of the most breathtaking scenery and vistas in England, and can always be tackled at a more leisurely pace by those with less experience or a lower level of fitness. Nevertheless, be warned that the steeper gradients may mean footwork for those not accustomed to strenuous climbs, and hence time allowance is needed to complete the route.

This guidebook is a complete companion to the route, which has been divided into six convenient and largely equal stages. Each stage opens with a route description, accompanied by a map and a diagram depicting the nature of the terrain encountered. Following this are greater details and illustrations of features along the way. This also includes useful accommodation details, particularly where cyclists are especially catered for, as well as food, drink and cycle shop facilities.

The entire route is not only covered, but also annotated, on the Ordnance Survey Yorkshire Dales Tourist Map 6, at the scale of 1 inch to 1 mile, thus making it the ideal map to carry.

THE YORKSHIRE DALES CYCLE WAY

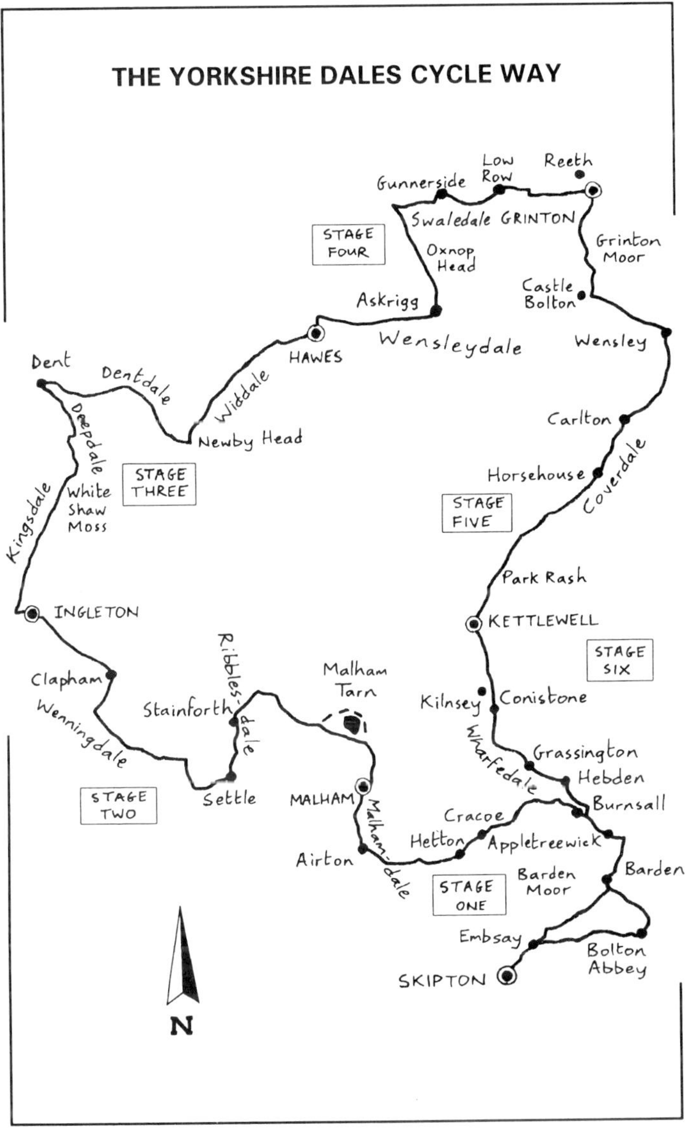

PREPARATION

The bicycle

A bicycle with high gearing for steep climbs is essential. Strong, efficient brakes for downhill sections are a must, as poor brakes could prove fatal: there are several descents where the gradient exceeds 20% in places. A mountain bike is not essential as most of the roads are well metalled but the low gearing on some of them may make steep climbs easier.

The following are the basic safety checks that should be made before setting off on every stage.

* Brake blocks should be checked for excessive wear and tear, and replaced if necessary.
* Brake and derailer cables should be adjusted so brakes are sharp and gears don't slip.
* Tyres inflated to manufacturer's recommended P.S.I. will puncture less easily.
* The seat should be adjusted to the correct level.

Equipment

Common sense and lightweight compactness is the rule. A basic list that you may wish to add to is set out below.

* Breathable waterproof outers - top and trousers.
* Warm and waterproof hat and gloves - the tops of many of the Dales are cold even in summer, and the weather on them can change extremely quickly all year round. Wind and rain combined give a wind-chill factor far exceeding the air temperature which may look quite benign on the weather reports.
* Reflective arm or body bands and bright clothing for night riding.
* Holmet marked with an approval sticker from a recognised body or institute.
* Front and rear lights and a rear reflector are legal requirements after dark.
* Basic toolkit to include pliers, multi-point screwdriver, adjustable spanner and bicycle pump.
* Puncture repair kit.
* Panniers are preferable to a rucksack for carrying your equipment, as the latter will de-stabilise you and obstruct your rear view if you have no rear view mirror.
* A rear view mirror is an excellent idea, and saves a lot of trouble in turning to view traffic approaching behind you. The number of riders who are not aware of traffic behind them is quite staggering. They are relatively cheap and simply attach to the handlebars.
* Although not equipment as such, training, even for those who consider themselves experienced, is a good idea and will improve road awareness, the most important factor in preventing accidents. Many local councils run safety training courses.

If camping, a modern powerful but lightweight gas stove is recommended if hot meals are thought to be essential, although the extra weight and space required may outweigh the convenience.

A fairly comprehensive guide to accommodation is given. The listings give facilities cyclists may find appropriate - a secure lock-up place for bikes and drying facilities are the commonest examples. They are given in capitals. If a listing has no such entries, this does not mean it won't have any suitable facilities: it may just be that the writer was unable to contact the owner direct, and details come from other sources. The best tactic is to book well in advance of the trip - an attempt has been made to cater for the budget cyclist in the addresses given, as this type of accommodation is scarcest of all.

Anyone prepared to pay over £12 per night should have few difficulties, as long as rooms are booked well in advance. Prices listed are for B & B for one person. A few official campsites exist, but enquiry at farmhouses offering bed and breakfast may result in an offer to camp in a field or at least the name of a local farmer who permits it. Also listed are a selection of eating establishments and cycle hire/repair shops. Please be aware that accommodation details - particularly prices - are liable to change at any time.

Access to the Way

Train is by far the best way to access the route, unless you wish to risk leaving a car in Skipton for the whole period, or live within cycling distance of the route itself. On Inter City lines it generally costs £3 per bike, while on local trains, carrying of bikes is usually at the discretion of the station master. It is best to check with the relevant stations in advance, particularly in the current rail 'climate'. Certainly at the time of writing British Rail were allowing cycles from Leeds and Manchester to Skipton at the above charge.

Organisations

• The Cyclists' Touring Club provide general information for the beginner. The CTC handbook is well worth obtaining for anyone who wishes to do any cycling nationally, as it contains national accommodation details as well as a list of bicycle repair shops. The handbook is £2.75 and full membership is £24, although there are various concession rates.

> Cyclists' Touring Club
> Cotterell House, 69 Meadrow, Godalming,
> Surrey GU7 3HS
> Tel. 01483 417217

• The Yorkshire Dales National Park supply a wealth of information on all matters relating to the area.

> Yorkshire Dales National Park Information Services
> Colvend, Hebden Road, Grassington, Skipton,
> North Yorkshire BD23 5LB
> Tel. 01756-752774

• Finally, why not consider becoming a member of the Yorkshire Dales Society? This worthy organisation acts as a watchdog and general good friend of the Dales.

> Yorkshire Dales Society
> Otley Civic Centre, Cross Green, Otley,
> West Yorkshire LS21 1HD
> Tel. 01943-461938

At the top of the High Street turn right alongside the castle wall. Take the first left slip for Embsay. This passes under road and railway bridges respectively then through Embsay and Eastby. Climb out of Eastby with Eastby Crag above you on the left, and past forestry plantations. Halton Height is the top of the climb, and offers a good view of Simon's Seat to the north-east across Wharfedale. At the T-junction after Lower Barden Reservoir turn left, then right immediately after Barden Tower and over Barden Bridge.

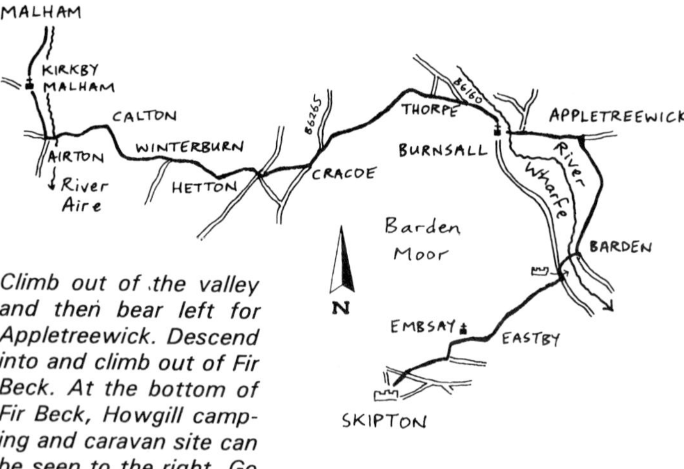

Climb out of the valley and then bear left for Appletreewick. Descend into and climb out of Fir Beck. At the bottom of Fir Beck, Howgill camping and caravan site can be seen to the right. Go left at the next junction into Appletreewick. A right turn would take you to Parceval Hall. Go through the village to Burnsall and then over the bridge right, towards Grassington on the B6160. Take the first left for Thorpe.

Bear right through Thorpe hamlet and then first left, marked as 'unsuitable for motor vehicles'. Meet the B6265 and go left into Cracoe, then right to Hetton. Here go right to Winterburn, then first right over the small bridge towards Calton. Bear left in the hamlet, to cross the river Aire and up into Airton. Go to the right of the green in Airton, and right at the T-junction. Passing through Kirkby Malham, go right at the T-junction, to Malham.

DISTANCE

36km

22 miles

GRADING

Moderate

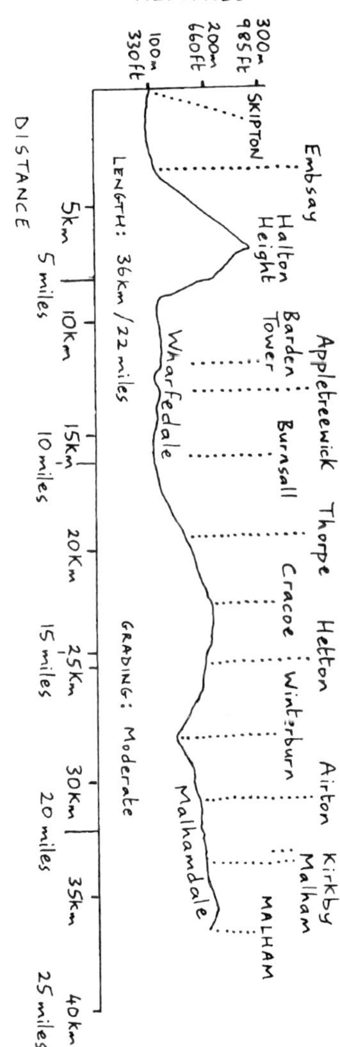

Skipton

Skipton Castle Dating from Norman times, the body of the subsequent medieval alterations to the castle has been substantially preserved, making it one of the finest examples of its kind in the whole country. Unusual and beautiful features are the yew tree in the central courtyard and the very impressive view of Skipton Woods to the north. The castle was the home of the powerful Cliffords, a northern family prominent in the nation's history throughout medieval times. The Tudor wing is now a cosy private residence.

> Admission: Adults £2.60; under 18's £1.30
> Opening times: Mon-Sat 10am-6pm (4pm Oct-Feb)
> Sun 2pm-6pm (4pm Oct-Feb)

Church of the Holy Trinity Many of the features of the church date from the fifteenth century or before. Intricate medieval architecture is clear from the roof, and the Clifford tombs show the strong connection between the church and nobility throughout the centuries. Henry, 1st Earl of Cumberland, an historical figure well known for his exploits on the Spanish main, is buried in one of the tombs. The good condition of both the castle and the church owe much to the expense and thought of Lady Anne Clifford, whose father is buried in the largest tomb to the right of the high altar.

Market days Monday, Wednesday, Friday, Saturday

Boat trips Between Easter and October, lasting over an hour on the Leeds-Liverpool Canal. Adults £2.50; children £1.50

Accommodation

Woolly Sheep Inn
38 Sheep Street
From £16
WASHING/DRYING FACILITIES

Large accommodation list to suit all pockets available from tourist information centre, 01756 792809
> Open Nov-March 10am-4pm (Sun 1pm-4pm)
> Apr-Oct 8am-5pm (Sun 2pm-5pm)

Food and drink

Royal Shepherd
Canal Street
Beers: Castle Eden, Cains,
Pedigree, Boddingtons

Woolly Sheep Inn
38 Sheep Street
Many meals under £5
Beers: Tetleys,Stones,guest beers
PACKED LUNCHES AVAILABLE

The Rose and Crown
Coach Street
Bar meals generally under £5, with Sunday carvery
Beers: Tetleys,guest beers   Folk night every Tuesday

Cycle shops

Cyclesport 2000
5 Water Street
01756 794386
Hire rates -
£10 per day
£40 per week

Dave Ferguson Cycles
1 Brook Street
01756 795376

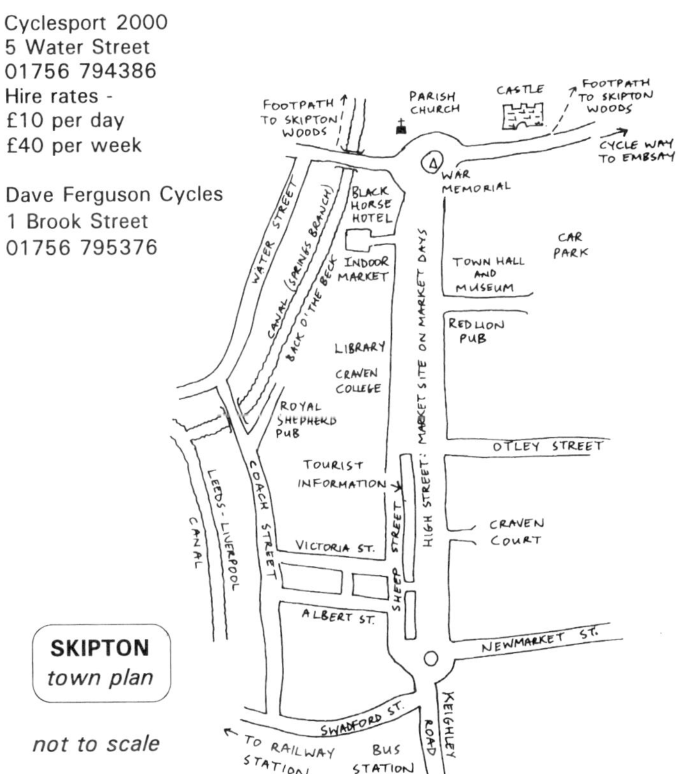

SKIPTON
town plan

not to scale

Embsay

A Brigantine bronze necklace discovered here suggests the village was once the site of a Celtic settlement. It was also the original site of what is now the remains of Bolton Abbey - moved, supposedly, lock, stock and barrel, at the wish of the Norman lady of the manor to commemorate the death of her son in the notorious Strid rapid - even then it seems people had the daring to attempt to leap across this potentially watery grave.

Embsay is now home to a privately owned steam railway, running a five mile return journey as follows:
Every Sunday throughout the year, Tuesdays and Saturdays in July, then daily from late July until the end of August

Accommodation   Rockwood House,   01756 799755

Food and drink   Elm Tree Inn,   Beers: Whitbread, guest beers

Barden Tower

Originally a 12th century hunting lodge, this impressive building is located next to the former hunting forest of Barden. Currently it is a crumbling ruin, undergoing work to prevent its collapse. It was used by the Norman aristocratic family the de Romilles, as well as providing shelter for locals when the Scots invaded Norman England. It passed to the hugely powerful Clifford family, and was rebuilt by Henry Clifford in 1523, and by Anne Clifford in 1658-9. Before it eventually fell into disuse, it served as an arms store for Jacobite rebels.

Accommodation

Hesketh House Farm
¾ mile from Bolton Abbey
01756 710332
£13-£16
SECURITY/DRYING FACILITIES

Howgill Lodge, Barden
01756 720665

Holme House Farm
near Barden
01756 720661

Barden Bunkhouse Barn
High Gamsworth Cottage
01756 720630

Appletreewick

There are good views from the hillside overlooking upper Wharfedale from Appletreewick. It is possible to visit the house and gardens at Parceval Hall nearby.

The Chapel of John the Baptist is a domestic looking building on the right as you enter the village. It is perhaps most notable for the carving bearing the mouse insignia of the famous Yorkshire woodcarver, Robert Thompson of Kilburn.

Accommodation

Blundellstead 01756 720632
Turn right as you approach the village centre on the downhill section

Camping

Masons camping and caravan site
At the bottom of the hill on the left as you leave Appletreewick

Food and Drink

New Inn
Enormous portions of traditional
food for around £5
Beers: John Smiths, Youngers,
and an amazing selection of
bottled foreign beers

Craven Heifer
Good variety of meals, £5-£10
Beers: Theakstons and
Boddingtons

Burnsall

This delightful Wharfedale village is centred around a beautiful bridge and spacious village green.

The church of St. Wilfrid   This historic site is named after a Bishop of York, who preached conversion from Paganism in Anglo-Saxon times, and founded the first church on the site of today's church. The church shows the influence of local noble patrons, notably the Norman de Romille family, whom the south-east chapel is named after.

On the masonry supporting the tower, look for the mason's mark 'Z', the same masons who worked on the priory church at Bolton Abbey. The church was restored in 1612 with the financial assistance of William Craven, a local who had made his fortune in London but decided to spend his wealth in his home community. Other notable features include the ancient font, probably Anglo-Saxon, while the coat of arms above the chancel is that of Edward VII.

In the graveyard look for the grave of William Bolton, once known as 'the Dales Minstrel', who was, amongst other things, a brilliant fiddler, knife grinder and casual labourer. When he died, stone broke, the local people were so attached to this colourful jack of all trades that they provided the money for a proper headstone, rather than the unmarked pauper's grave that would have been common at this time.

Accommodation

Conistone House
01756 720650

Manor House Private Hotel
01756 720231

Burnsall

St. Wilfrid's,
Burnsall

Thorpe

The hamlet of Thorpe nestles hidden between two limestone knolls, and still has today the feeling of isolation that protected it in centuries past from marauding Scottish invaders.

Accommodation

Holly Tree Farm   01756 720604   £15

Cracoe and Hetton

Camping

Threaplands House Farm, Cracoe
01756 730248

Food and Drink

Devonshire Arms
Cracoe
Beers: Youngers

The Angel Inn, Hetton
£19-£30 for three courses,
including wine and coffee:
an up-market establishment

Airton

If approached on a sunny day, the gently rolling, pastoral country before Airton takes on an almost luminescent greenness, before the road drops away to reveal the picture postcard view over the upper Aire.

Accommodation

Woodland Cottage
01729 830572

Airton Quaker Hostel
The Nook
01729 830263

Mrs W.P. Hoare
The Green
01729 830451

Lindon Guest House
01729 830418   £17
SECURITY/DRYING FACILITIES

Kirkby in Malhamdale (Kirkby Malham)

The church in this quiet village is steeped in history. Near the south-east buttress the coat of arms of Fountains Abbey is displayed - a blue background with three silver horseshoes - along with the crests of local aristocratic benefactors. The font is of uncertain date, but doubtless of great antiquity. The sanctuary shows good examples of continental glasswork along with an intricately carved Morrison memorial, the local M.P. for Skipton in the early twentieth century. The elaborate pews show Jacobean design.

Accommodation

Victoria Inn
01729 830213
£16 and over

Kirkby Malham

Malham

Unfortunately, good weather means the village of Malham resembles the site of a pilgrimage, and if an overnight stop is planned it may be necessary for the budget cyclist to book months in advance in order to use the only reasonably cheap accommodation.

Accommodation

Hilltop Farm Bunkbarn
Malham
01729 830320
£6

Beck Hall
Malham
01729 830332

Capon Hall Cottage
Malham Moor
01729 830476
£16
SECURITY/DRYING FACILITIES

Lister Arms
01729 830330
£20
SECURITY/DRYING FACILITIES

Friars Garth
Malham
01729 830328

Camping

Townhead Farm
01729 830310

Gordale Scar House
01729 830333

*Gordale Scar,
Malham*

LIVING HISTORY IN THE MALHAM AREA

Age of the Barbarians and the Norman Invasion

After being freed from Roman rule, the unlucky Britons found themselves, after two hundred years of freedom, threatened by a new and seemingly more terrible foe. Anglo-Saxon invasion was the direct product of the displacement of tribes right across Europe, whose origin lay in the fear caused by ravaging Huns moving west from Asia.

British history prior to the establishment of Anglo-Saxon kingdoms is as much romantic mythology as fact - peopled by such hazy figures as Arthur and Uther Pendragon, supposed inhabitant of Mallerstang.

As had happened in Celtic Britain, and was to happen again in Norman Britain, a period of terrible devastation and human misery gave way to the establishment of centres of religious learning and culture. Peace and prosperity bred the wealth which allowed monastic endowments to be made, and Britain was no longer the savage perimeter zone on the edge of the known world but, briefly, an exporter of religious faith and culture.

Malham Cove

The eighth and ninth centuries saw the historical wheel take another turn, with the ingress of Danes and later Norse Vikings bringing bloodshed succeeded by peace that was at the expense of the extinction of monasticism. The Danes saw monasteries simply as 'regional safe deposits'. The northern Scandinavian empire would have been all the more powerful and potentially creative were it not for the constant internecine expeditions of Dublin based Vikings to conquer York Vikings and vice versa.

The strongest legacy of Viking invasion today lies in the place names of the upper dales - suffixes thwaite, sett, side, wick, kirk, thorpe and the Yorkshire word for a brook - beck. Leys, tons and hams are generally of Anglo-Saxon origin.

Prior to Norman invasion the destiny of the Dales could have been pulled in a number of different directions, most probably some form of independent Northern kingdom ruled either by native, Scottish or Scandinavian rulers. In the final event the Norman presence of William the Conqueror made itself felt in the most violent way possible. Risings of the native thanes were put down in 1068 and 1069 by a process known (with great understatement) as the Harrying of the North.

In order to destroy the power base of native leaders and prevent further Scandinavian invasions, William the Conqueror pursued a scorched earth policy, in other words a widespread campaign of agricultural destruction and depopulation. A contemporary chronicler records how the roads of the dales were littered with dead bodies which attracted hungry wolves from the fells.

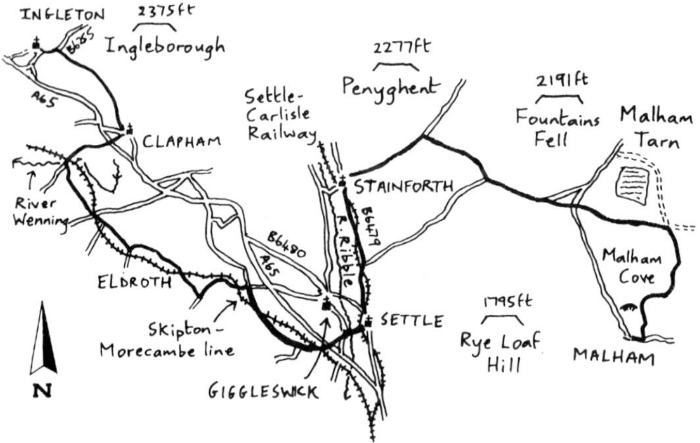

In Malham village turn first right over the bridge, then left after the Post office and youth hostel, signposted for Malham Tarn. The hard climb over Malham Rakes and towards Settle is rewarded by surreal limestone pavement scenery. Alternative routes pass in front of or behind the tarn. The latter, an unmetalled track, offers the best views of this glacial lake. This bridleway behind the tarn is also the Pennine Way.

The main route swings left over the outflow of the tarn, and on to a T-junction by Sannat Hall. Turn left for Stainforth, and there turn left again to Settle. Turn right after the second pedestrian crossing (passing the market square en route). Go under the railway bridge (Settle-Carlisle) and past the railway station. Go over the river Ribble and a minor crossroads on the edge of Giggleswick, and after crossing the A65 Settle by-pass go under another railway bridge (Skipton-Morecambe).

Remain on the 'main' road as far as a crossroads, then bear left through Eldroth. Two kilometres further, bear left to a T-junction under a railway bridge, where you then turn right for Clapham. There are good views now across to the north, of the limestone uplands and of Ingleborough's profile.

Go right at the next T-junction, passing under the railway again at Clapham station, and cross the A65 with care to enter the village of Clapham. Follow the stream up through the village, keeping to the left of it. At the top turn sharp left, then right at the next junction. The old Clapham-Ingleton road brings the stage to an end. Just on the edge of Ingleton, turn left down the B6255 into the village, going right for the centre.

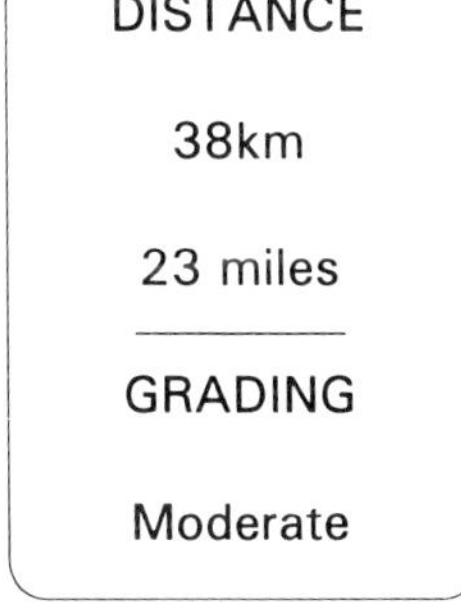

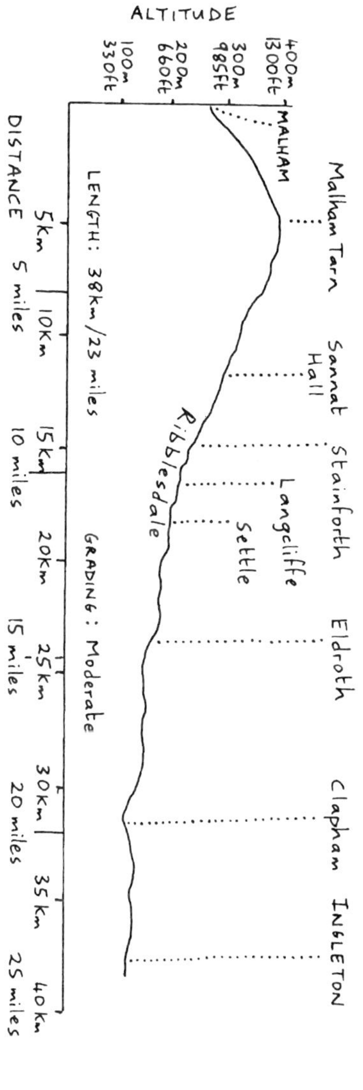

DISTANCE

38km

23 miles

GRADING

Moderate

LIVING HISTORY AROUND MALHAM TARN

The founding of the monasteries

Large feudal estates were built up to fortify the area against the threat of Scottish invasion, and the Battle of the Standard in 1138 saw off the major Scottish threat. Military entrenchment was allied with the growth of religious wealth and culture, most notably in the form of Cistercian monks. They were reformed monks, less allied to the 'parasitic' Benedictine monks associated with traditional landed wealth, and sought to create and produce through their own labours. They created the abbeys whose remains can be seen on the route at Jervaulx and Coverham, and became perhaps the most important contributors to the wealth of Norman England. At Fountains Abbey lay the heartland of wool production in Europe, and the powerhouse of the medieval European economy. Sheep were brought 25 miles over green tracks from Fountains to the rich pastures above Malham.

Stainforth

Accommodation

Youth Hostel
Taitlands
Stainforth
01729 823577

Food and drink

Craven Heifer
Stainforth
Beers: Thwaites

Camping

Knight Stainforth Hall
Little Stainforth
01729 822200
WC, showers, laundry, farm produce, telephone
Open March-October

Packhorse bridge, Stainforth

26

Settle

Like Skipton, Settle is still recognisably in form and character a market town, perhaps with even less of a gloss of twentieth century large scale commercialism. The place derives its name from the Anglo-Saxon 'a dwelling place', and along with Skipton became one of the great centres of the Dales pastoral economy, with the decline of cottage industries from the late eighteenth century onwards. It had, however, always been fairly isolated until the building of the Keighley - Kendal turnpike in the 1750's. Huge herds of cattle were brought by drovers down from Scotland to be sold at Settle and Skipton markets.

The town also marks the starting point of the Settle to Carlise railway, passing through some of the most wildly beautiful countryside in England. The line was a monumental feat of human labour when constructed from 1869 to 1876. There is a regular passenger service and occasionally steam locomotives haul up the 'Long Drag', the first 20 miles from Settle. Pictures of this magnificent sight adorn many of the pubs in the area.

The Watershed Mill is a noteworthy piece of architecture - a former textile mill beside the Langcliffe road that has been converted into a crafts centre.

The imaginative and eclectic nature of Settle's architecture can be appreciated using the map set out on page 29.

A LOOK AT OLD SETTLE

1 THE SHAMBLES - The name dates back to the time when this multi-storied, arched building housed butchers shops. Built in the seventeenth century originally as a market hall, in the eighteenth century arches and the cottages were added.

2 FOUNTAIN PILLAR - replaced an earlier market cross that had been on this site for centuries

3 TOWN HALL - built in 1833

4 CHEAPSIDE - an interesting row of small business premises

5 NAKED MAN CAFE - named as a satirical comment on the local fashions at the time of its construction

6 BISHOPDALE COURT - note Bishopdale House, of seventeenth century limestone construction

7 ASHFIELD HOUSE - now a social club, but originally built in the nineteenth century by the founder of the Craven Bank

8 VICTORIA HALL - built in 1853 as a music hall

9 FRIENDS MEETING HOUSE - built in 1689 and acknowledged as the first in the area

10 POLICE STATION - formerly Cragdale House, built by a local solicitor

11 MUSEUM OF NORTH CRAVEN LIFE

12 PRIMROSE FARM - note the ancient datestone built into the building

13 THE FOLLY - formerly Tanner Hall, the residence of a wealthy Tanner. Of mid seventeenth century construction

14 WELL STEPS and STONE TROUGHS

15 ZION CHURCH - built in 1816

Victoria Cave,
Settle

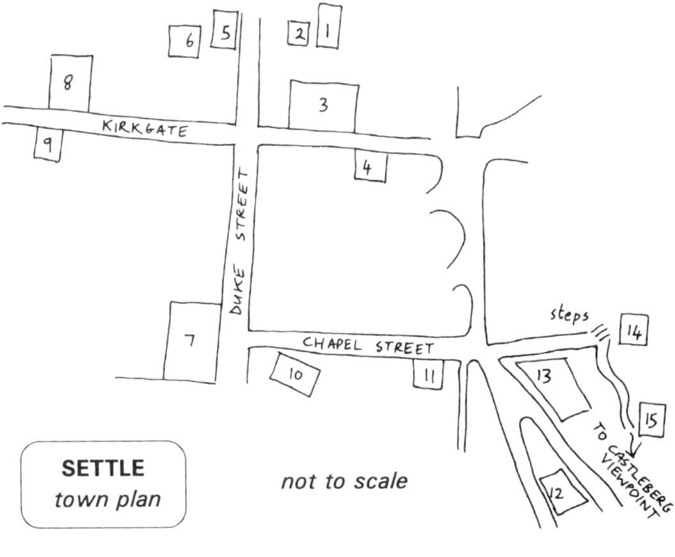

SETTLE
town plan

not to scale

Accommodation

Harts Head Hotel
Belle Hill
Giggleswick
01729 882086
£20
SECURE/DRYING FACILITIES

Sansbury Vegetarian Guest House
Sansbury Place
50 Duke Street
01729 82384
£17
SECURE/DRYING FACILITIES

Yorkshire Dales Field Centre
(Bunkbarn)
17 Church Street
Giggleswick
01729 822965/824180

The Oast Guest House
5 Pen-y-Ghent View
01729 822989
£13-£16

Penmar Court Guest House
Duke Street
01729 823258
£14-£15
SECURE/DRYING FACILITIES

Chalimbana Cottage
3 Ribble Terrace
01729 823988
£14.50
SECURE/DRYING FACILITIES

Grain House Farm (Camping Barn)   01200 28366

Food and drink

Harts Head Hotel
Bar meals generally under £5
Beers: Taylors, Tetleys, Boddingtons, Castle Eden

Little House Food and Wine Bar
Kirkgate
Snacks and Meals £5-£10

Naked Man Cafe
Market Place
Snacks, sandwiches and light meals under £5

Royal Oak
Market Place
Most meals £5-£15
Beer: Whitbread

Cycle shop   Settle Cycles, Duke Street   01729 22216

The route skirts the south-western edge of the Dales, going past the village of Giggleswick and through Clapham. A scenic walk northwards from Clapham allows a more adventurous ascent of Ingleborough than the well trodden path from Ingleton. Giggleswick's principal function is to provide education for the inhabitants of Settle, although it also boasts the ancient church of St. Alkelda. Amongst other treasures are Tempest effigies and a 17th century pulpit. Settle's 19th century church com-memorates victims of the Settle-Carlise railway in its porch.

Clapham

The village straddles Clapham Beck, which starts life emerging at Ingleborough Cave and drops with a rush over a waterfall at the back of the church of St James. The church itself is built on the line of the Craven Fault. The church was virtually rebuilt in 1814 with the ends of former Jacobean pews now panelling the walls.

Ingleborough Cave Access is along a 2 mile nature trail and a leaflet is available from the National Park Centre in Clapham. It extends a quarter of a mile into the hillside and access is gained through the picturesque valley of Clapdale. The mouth to the cave was previously blocked by a large stalagmite broken in 1837, and the water backing up and filling the cave was drained to reveal the formations. For the footpath go to the north of the village on the cycle route past the church, and follow the signposts.
Guided tours, 1st March - 31st October
015242 51242

Accommodation

New Inn
Clapham
015242 51203
Over £22

Brook House
Station Road
015242 51580
£13-£16

Camping

Flying Horseshoe Hotel
Clapham Station
015242 51229

Ingleton

Impressively set on a ledge overlooking the rivers Doe and Twiss, Ingleton is the main access point for Ingleborough (723m, 2372 ft). The peak claims historical romanticism as it was here the Celtic Brigantine leader Venutius rallied his troops before leading them against his betraying wife, who had sold out the Celts by making a pact with the Roman invaders.

Beezley and Snow falls are among the impressive and relentlessly promoted waterfalls, while the easiest and most popular footpath to the summit of Ingleborough lies to the east. Caving - along with abseiling - remains popular (Freetime Activities 01539 62828). White Scar Cave, 1 ½ miles away, is the largest show cave in England. It is open 10am-5.30pm (last tour)

St. Mary's church has perhaps the most dramatic setting of any church in the Dales, nestling paternalistically above the smoking chimneys of the village. Often rebuilt, the church retains a Norman font and tower, the latter with narrative carvings.

Accommodation- comprehensive list from tourist office, 015242 41049

Craven Heifer Inn
Main Street
015242 41427
£14
SECURE/DRYING FACILITIES,
PACKED LUNCHES

Dale Bank Guest House
Back Square
015242 41986
£12.50
SECURE/DRYING FACILITIES,
PACKED LUNCHES

Ingleborough View Guest House
Main Street
015242 41523
£14
SECURE/DRYING FACILITIES,
PACKED LUNCHES

Wheatsheaf Hotel
High Street
015424 41275
£14
SECURE/DRYING FACILITIES,
PACKED LUNCHES

The Barnstead Bunkhouse
Stacksteads Farm
Ingleton
015242 41386
Kitchen facilities, WC's, showers
£6

Gatehouse Farm
Far Westhouse
015242 41458/41307
£15
SECURE/DRYING FACILITIES,
PACKED LUNCHES

Ingleton Youth Hostel, Greta Tower, Ingleton 015242 41444

Camping

Enter Farm
Enter Lane
New Road
Ingleton
015242 41464
WC, washing

Moorgarth Farm
New Road
Ingleton
015242 41428
WC, hot showers

Food and Drink

The Copper Kettle
High Street
Snacks under £5

Inglevorough

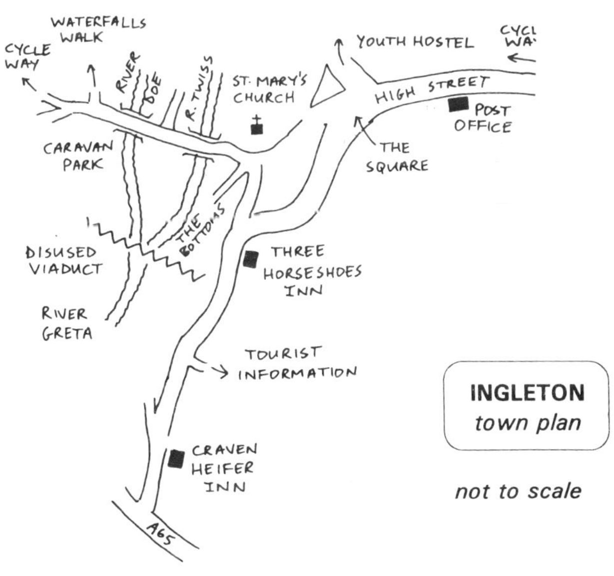

From the town centre, a road forks off left as you ascend the Main Street past the tourist office. Take this, drop down and then up, going left over two bridges and finally under the old viaduct. Fork right, then right again into Thornton in Lonsdale. Turn right past the church and climb for between 6 and 7 kilometres to the gate at Kingsdale Head. There are impressive views of the millstone grit capped mountains towering above, with Whernside on the right on the ascent. Continue over the top of White Shaw Moss, dropping down into Deepdale.

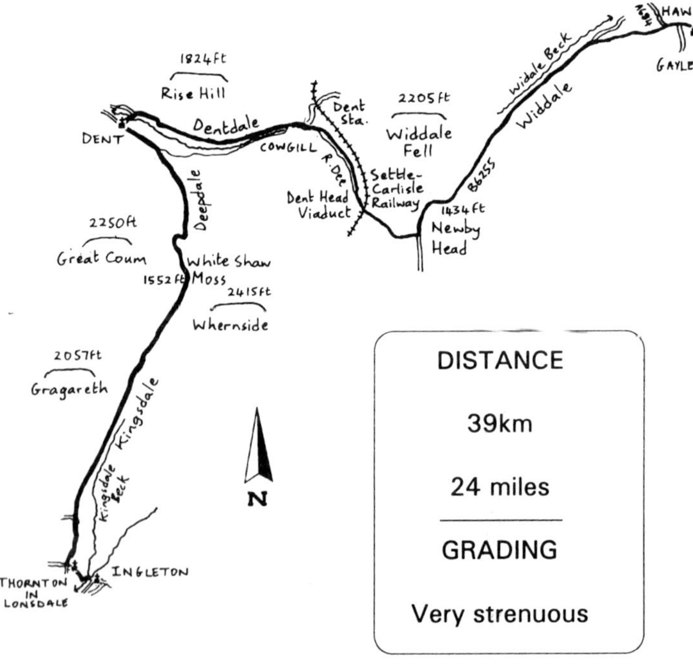

DISTANCE

39km

24 miles

GRADING

Very strenuous

Descending into Deepdale, dismount at the 20% sign. An impressive waterfall is passed about half-way down, on the left. Pass through the tiny hamlet of Slack, and then turn left at the T-junction signposted for Dent. Continue into the town centre. At the main junction in the centre is the Sedgwick memorial stone. Here follow the signpost for Hawes. The church is on your left as you exit, shortly before passing over the river Dee. The road sweeps gradually to the right to follow the floor of Dentdale.

Continue on past Ewegales Bridge (the road leads back to Dent on the other side of the river) and past a left for Dent station and Garsdale Head. Climb by the Sportsman's Inn and past Dent Head Viaduct. At Newby Head go left onto the B6255, and continue for 6 miles to the junction with the A684. Turn right into Hawes centre, past the youth hostel on the edge of town.

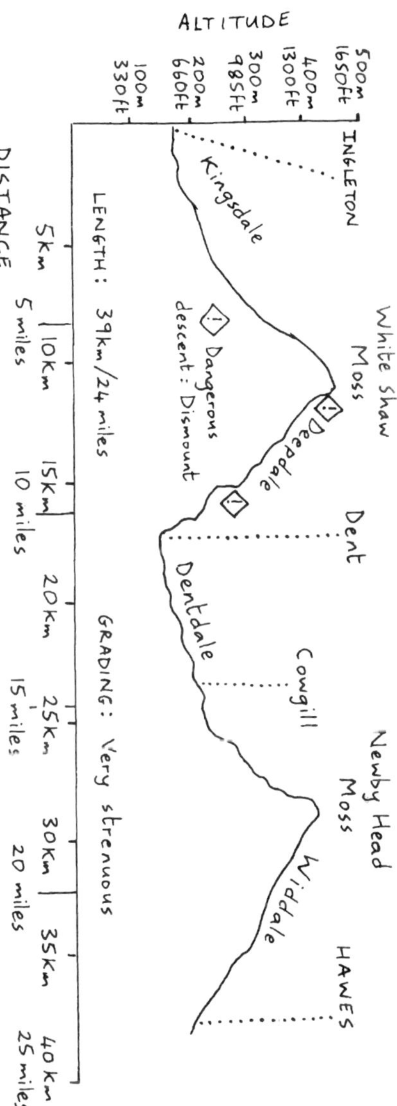

Thornton Force

Kingsdale

The valley floor initially possesses a strange geometric design, but the uniformity of the climb gives way to more strenuous gradients after Kingsdale Head. The effort is well rewarded by the spectacular views of Deepdale once over White Shaw Moss. Further down Deepdale, waterfalls decorate the valley side, and idyllic footpaths lead off alongside Deepdale Beck.

Great Coum from White Shaw Moss

Dent

The village is so perfectly preserved it could almost be an historical filmset. A combination of Lakeland gaiety and the understated Dales fastness gives the village its real charm. Only the presence of cars on its narrow streets shatter the illusion one is in the seventeenth or eighteenth century (around which time many of the houses are dated by inscription above their doors). Previously the houses had first floor galleries constructed into them, and in the days of the 'knitting industry', whole families would gather to knit on the galleries.

Church Bridge, Dent

The church of St. Andrew As usual the local aristocracy, in the form of the Sedgwick family, are commemorated here in stained glass. The seventeenth and eighteenth century pews are found to be personalised with the initials of local sidesmen, presiding parishioners, illustrating a system still working today. The Sill memorial on the far wall as you enter commemorates the local Sill brothers who made their fortunes from employing West African slaves on their West Indian sugar plantations. Their building of the local Whernside Manor with the profits aroused much moral controversy amongst the Dent villagers.

The chancel floor is paved with Dent marble, showing the beauty and quality of the product of this local industry before its sad decline. The beautiful east window illustrates an elaborate song of praise to God, showing a profusion of angels and saints. The windows in the south aisle are memorials to the Sedgwicks. Adam, the most famous, is commemorated in the memorial stone in the central village square, the foremost geologist of his day.

The valley is home to Dent Brewery, one of the remotest in the country. It sells its beers at both the Sun Inn and George & Dragon in Dent itself.

At the top of Flinter Gill are old limestone workings, previously used to make fireplaces.

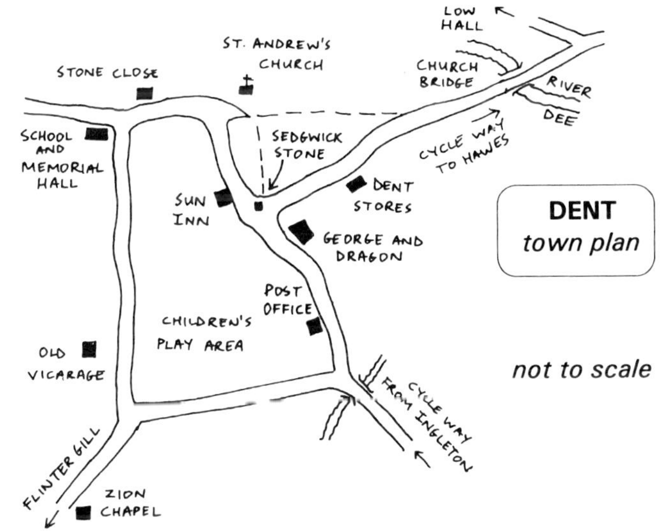

Accommodation

Stone Close
Main Street
015396 25231
£13-£16

The Barn
Womans' Land
015396 25265
Under £13
SECURE/DRYING FACILITIES

Camping

High Laning Farm
015396 25239

Food and Drink

Stone Close
Main Street
Dent
£11-£17 for 3 courses,
including wine and coffee

Dent Stores/
Garda View House
015396 25209
£13-£16

Low Hall Farm
first left after bridge
after exiting Dent

Cycle hire

The North Country shop
The Filling Station
015875 460

Sun Inn
Main Street
Meals around £5
Beers: Dent Brewery, also served
at the George and Dragon

39

LIVING HISTORY IN DENT

The growth of the great northern industries and the cottage decline

The growth of coal mining increasingly centred upon the urban areas on the peripheries of the Dales. Allied with this was the growth of textile mills, notably producing cotton. These, together with cheaper foreign imports such as continental lead, effectively killed off various traditional aspects of Dales life.

Relatively small scale industries such as lead mining, and cottage industries such as knitting woollens, perished before monolithic industrialisation and foreign importation. At one time, in villages such as Dent, it was said the sound of knitting needles used by all generations, male and female alike, drowned out all other sound. Lead mining, once a supplement to the farmer's income, saw skilled workers either emigrate or being pushed into the appalling conditions of the mines. The ghostly remnants of this activity can be seen above the town of Grassington and in upper Swaledale, both on the route of the Cycle Way.

Dent Town

A decreasing number of traditional farmers found themselves supplying the swelling northern conurbations, and shifting from arable to pastoral farming - a relationship still very much in evidence today. The population of Swaledale, for example, is only a quarter of what it was 150 years ago.

The landscape was changed still more profoundly with the growth of turnpike and eventually tarmaced roads. The railways also opened up the countryside to curious Victorians, many imbued with a serious intellectual interest in the abundant nature - far different from today's blatant commercial tourism. The Settle to Carlisle railway was completed by an army of navvies working in appalling conditions, many of whom have only the grandeur of the viaducts left as their epitaphs.

Bridges of two ages:
Viaduct and packhorse
at Dent Head

Dentdale

The dale climbs slowly against the run of the tumbling stream, starting from Church Bridge just outside Dent to Dent Head Viaduct. High and Low chapel in the lower vale once belonged to Coverham Abbey. During the Reformation, a pitched battle was fought here by tenants against the King's agents sent to repossess Church lands. Nearby Broadfield House was once the home of the owners of Stonehouse marbleworks, until the industry was killed off by cheap Italian imports.

The whole of the dale testifies to the strength of the independent churches and the independence of the Dales people, who had the courage to defy the powerful and at times merciless state. The elevated chapel started life as one of five Methodist chapels built in the dale. Quaker houses flourished, such as those known as Fletchers and Hobsons. George Fox, the nationally famous anti-Catholic spirit, toured the dale preaching to locals in 1652. The hamlet of Cowgill itself nestles in the peace of upper Dentdale and houses the Chapel of St. John the Evangelist. It is of strikingly simple design with lancet windows.

Accommodation

Scow Cottage
Cowgill
015396 25445
£13-£16
SECURE/DRYING FACILITIES

Birk Rigg
Cowgill
015396 25367
£13-£16
SECURE/DRYING FACILITIES

Dentdale Youth Hostel
Cowgill
015396 25251

The Sportsman's Inn
Cowgill
015396 25282
£17-£19
SECURE/DRYING FACILITIES
BY PRIOR ARRANGEMENT

Camping

Ewegales Farm
(right at Ewegales Bridge
 just before Cowgill)

Food and drink

Harbourgill Farm
Cowgill
015396 25392

The Sportsman's Inn
Cowgill
Bar meals from under £5-£10
Beers: Theakstons and Youngers

LIVING HISTORY IN THE DENT AREA

Enclosure and the rise of the landed gentry

The late eighteenth century witnessed the rise of enclosure: the system of open fields was replaced with the now familiar dry stone walls which date from this period. As cottage industry was replaced by mass industrialisation, so small scale farming was replaced by larger fields, gradually enclosed by an increasingly small and powerful group of landowners. As did the 'terrible knitters of Dent' (so called for their speed and productivity at hand knitting) so the local tenant farmers left in increasing numbers to find work in the cities, or as labourers on farms elsewhere.

Behind the physical phenomenon lay the change in social structure from smaller tenant farmers to larger landowning families, fuelled by changes brought about by the agricultural revolution and statutes enabling enclosure to take place. The smaller farmers were squeezed by onerous taxation which left those who could afford it to capitalise and enlarge their estates. Such groups became powerfully active in Parliament, through the operation of a very effective and unashamedly self interested group of landowners headed by Christopher Wyvill, who formed his own infamous land league. The amassing of landed wealth was in some cases supplemented or exceeded by the exploitation of mining on a large scale.

Some time later, this landed wealth was to confront the 'noveau riche' of the industrial revolution who demanded parliamentary representation.

This period also saw a significant depopulation of the Dales - a process further accelerated by the arrival of the industrial revolution in earnest. The new urban centres removed from the land the excess labour force created by enclosure.

Bridge End, Dent Head

Hawes

The beck running through Hawes and its smaller neighbour Gayle gives both these villages much of their character, even if some of that character is subsumed at peak season by tourism. The twisting streets of the eastern parts of the town centre reveal new vistas of the old buildings at every turn.

Much of the history of this market town is related in the Dales Countryside Museum. The interweaving of livestock farming, cheese production and lead mining is clearly demonstrated. The museum is undergoing a major expansion scheme and will include a specialised local studies centre.

The town was connected by rail to eastern Wensleydale in the nineteenth century and the line subsequently closed. There is at present a campaign to re-open the line.

Hawes is a very large exporter of milk, and 6000 gallons go to London every day from upper Wensleydale. Wensleydale cheese is the town's most famous product, and is today made on a large commercial scale, not as previously by farmers' wives in hand presses. Its recent closure was a disastrous prospect for the people of Hawes, but happily a buy-out has seen activity return, and with it many local jobs. The Wensleydale creamery on Gayle Lane now caters for visitors who wish to see how cheese is made. There is also a ropemakers near the old station yard open to the public.

Livestock is traded at the auction mart at the eastern end of the town, although this trading has lost much of the colour it had when held in the open in the market square.

Countryside Museum
Open   April - October 10am-5pm
         Occasional weekend winter opening

Market day   Tuesday

Events   The Wensleydale Advertiser will have details of local events and is available at local newsagents

Accommodation

A list of accommodation may be pinned outside the market on the notice board. Hawes tourist office (01969 667450) has a list of accommodation, and there is an electronic information point in the wall of the old stationmaster's house in Station Yard.

Hawes Youth Hostel
Lancaster Terrace
01969 667368

White Hart Inn
Main Street
01969 667529
£16.50

Pry House
01969 667241
£12.50

Old Chapel, Cotterdale
£11.50

Stonehouse Hotel
Sedbusk
01969 667338
£25
SECURITY/DRYING/WASHING

Laburnum House
The Holme
01969 667717
£15

Ivy Deane
The Holme
£13.50

The Old Station House
01969 667785
£17.50

Board Hotel
Market Place
01969 667223
£18

Halfway House
01969 667442
£13

Camping

Bainbridge Ings
Hawes
01969 667345
WC, showers, laundry, shop

Brown Moor Farm
Hawes 01969 667338
WC, showers, shop, laundry

Shaw Ghyll
Camping and Caravan Site
Simonstone, near Hawes
01969 667359
WC only

Food and Drink

Board Hotel, Market Place
Bar Meals - lunch, tea and dinner from £3
Beers: Jennings Bitter and Cumberland Ale

1 THE MARKET HALL

This is the heart of Hawes. The building was the result of a generous gift of money left in a local resident's will. Public subscription was also used to finish construction of the building in the late nineteenth century. On Tuesdays the hall accommodates traders' stalls as well as the resident library. The market hall also acts as a social centre for local clubs.

2 COCKETT'S

This was previously a Quaker meeting house. It was used to accommodate members of the Society of Friends who would come from all over the dale to attend meetings here. The carved words over the front door read 'God being with us who can be against us. A.T.F.A.D. 1668'

3 KIT CALVERT'S SECOND-HAND BOOKSHOP

This is found up the first ginnel after the market hall and on the left (proceeding away from the youth hostel and primary school). The shop has a good selection of books on all topics, including local history.

'THE NEUKIN'

Near Barclays Bank, between the Black Bull Cafe and 'Specials', is an opening still known as the Neukin. It is famous in village history as the place where an old widow kept a lodging house catering for tramps, giving them bed, tea and bread & dripping for 4d a night. It also housed colourful characters and temporary joiners and other tradesmen in the town's boom days.

4 BARCLAYS BANK

This neo-Jacobean style building was home to a local bank.

5 MIDLAND BANK (with cash point)

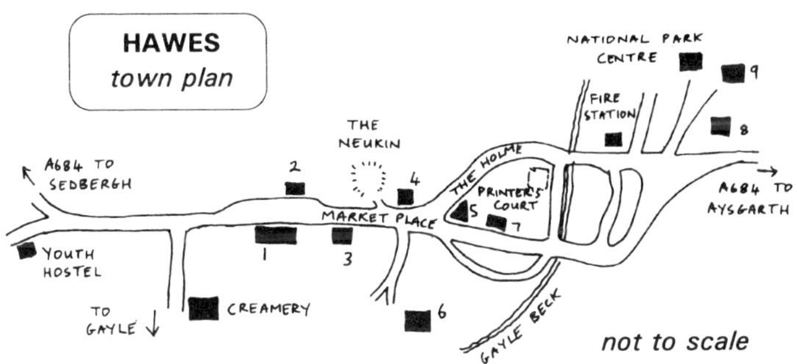

6 ST. MARGARET'S CHURCH

This relatively new church was constructed in 1851. A full guide is published and available inside the building. Behind the church, in the first graveyard, stands the Hawes Junction memorial. It commemorates a 1910 accident at Lunds on the Settle-Carlisle railway, when twelve passengers were killed. Both fields in which the graveyards are contained have many unmarked graves, many of them navvies who worked on the railway and never earned enough to afford the vestiges of a decent funeral.

7 THE WHITE HART INN

This is an old coaching inn and stage post office. The inn was most popular with travellers in the early nineteenth century before the real emergence of the railways as the popular means of mass transport. The bell on the side of the inn was to summon fresh horses from the stables which were opposite, when the coach was ready to leave.

PRINTER'S COURT

This is beautifully evocative of Hawes' bygone days, and the total enclosure of the court adds to the feeling of being in the past. This was previously the home of the Hawes newspaper. The 'local' has since moved to Burtersett Road.

8 HAWES ROPEMAKERS

9 DALES COUNTRYSIDE MUSEUM

Exit Hawes on the main road east towards Askrigg, and take an immediate left for Hardraw Force just before the museum in Station Yard. Continue over the bridge to turn right at the T-junction for Askrigg. Follow the valley side into Askrigg, the road gently rolling along with the variations in rock strata that make up the valley side.

Through Askrigg town centre take a left, signposted Muker, and climb over the top of Askrigg Common. The climb out of Askrigg is steep, and low gearing is very useful. Above and to your right on the ascent looms Ellerkin Scar, protecting the grouse shooting moors that are nowadays big business. The road rises sharply over the first cattle-grid, and the rolling heather clad peat moor eases into view.

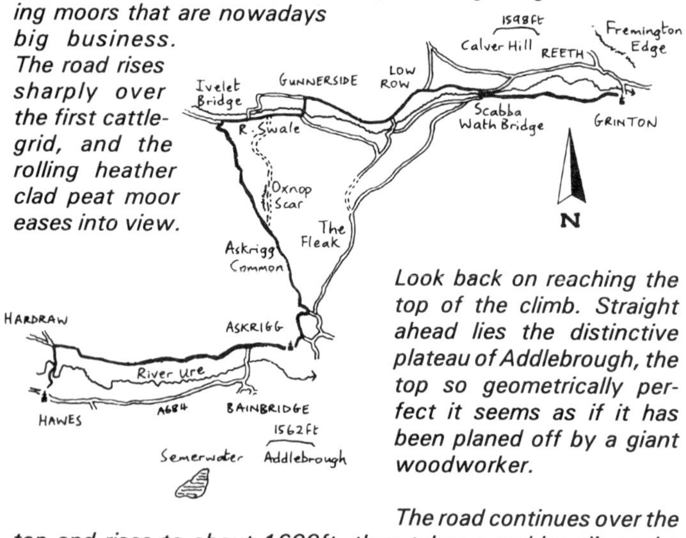

Look back on reaching the top of the climb. Straight ahead lies the distinctive plateau of Addlebrough, the top so geometrically perfect it seems as if it has been planed off by a giant woodworker.

The road continues over the top and rises to about 1600ft, then takes a sudden dip and a twist before passing the impressive limestone of Oxnop Scar on the right. The vistas on the descent are stunning on a clear day. To the right Satron Moor twists and bumps its descent to the valley floor. Further round the valley side to the east were some of the most productive lead mines in Swaledale. Various farm buildings perch on the shoulder of the moor, and straight ahead lies Rogan's Seat. The second footpath after Oxnop Farm short-cuts to the Cycle Way on the valley, and is a short picturesque walk. The former mining villages of Thwaite and Muker nestle at the feet of smaller valleys.

At the bottom of the descent, turn right at the T-junction and continue into Satron and over the river into Gunnerside.
BEWARE:
THE DESCENT IS EXTREMELY STEEP BEFORE THE ROAD JUNCTION AT CROW TREES - DISMOUNT BEFORE DESCENDING.

Continue through Low Row and Feetham, crossing the river about a mile out of Feetham and continue down the valley into Grinton.

DISTANCE
30km
18 miles
GRADING
Strenuous

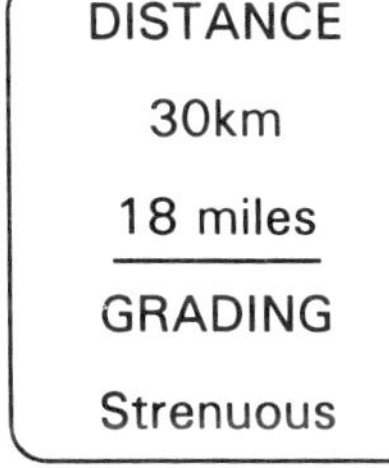

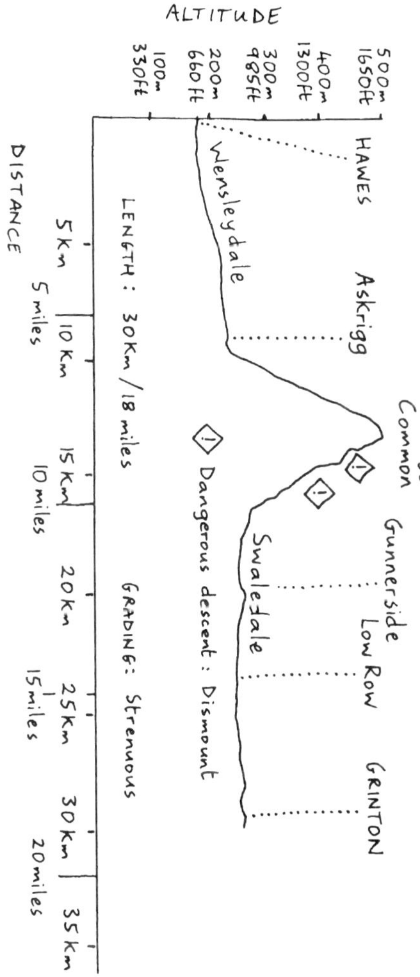

Wensleydale

On exiting Hawes it is obvious why it became such an important pass through the more rugged western end of Wensleydale. To the west, Widdale Fell rises on the far side of the valley to 2000 feet. To the east on the right is High Abbotside Common, so called because it was in the former ownership of Jervaulx Abbey, further down the dale. A good view is afforded down the valley, as the Ure begins to wind its course that will see it join the Ouse and eventually make its way into the Humber.

Askrigg

Most famous because of its links with the televising of the James Herriot novels, Askrigg is a beautiful market town in its own right. Originally, Askrigg was *the* market town of Wensleydale, until the granting of a market charter to Hawes, which soon came to overshadow its eastern neighbour in commercial success and size if not in beauty. Because it subsequently had to play second fiddle to Hawes in terms of economic growth, Askrigg has retained more of its traditional character and intimacy.

Traditionally, clockmaking was the industry here, but the advent of cheaper, American-made clocks in the nineteenth century all but emaciated this industry. As in most other Dales villages, Askrigg now relies on the twin industries of agriculture and tourism for the bulk of its income.

Askrigg Hill Fair takes place annually in the Market Place, though only a shadow of the original fair. This was once the major annual event of the village, centring on the exhibition and selling of horses between men from Wensleydale and Swaledale. Often pure equine interest was mixed with mutual hostility and pride, and the event could end in fights between men of the different dales. The event had such a following that it once attracted horse traders from Scotland. Legend has it that one of these Scottish traders was murdered by Askrigg farmers, and witnesses to the crime were hushed up by the guilty. Grinton parish register certainly records the finding of a body upon the peat moors by a farmer digging the turf for fuel.

Accommodation

Thornsgill Guest House
Moor Road
01969 650617
Under £18.50
SECURE/DRYING FACILITIES

Mrs. B. Percival
Milton House
01969 650217
Under £15
SECURE FACILITIES

Sykes House
01969 650535
£14
SECURE/DRYING FACILITIES

West Lea
01969 650479
£14
SECURE/DRYING FACILITIES

Food and drink

Crown Inn
Beers: John Smiths,
Youngers, Theakstons

Rowan Tree Restaurant
Set Menu - over £18

Cycle hire

Ian Rawlins
Woodburn Garage - next to Crown Inn
01969 650455

*Nappa Hall, Askrigg -
a 15th century
fortified manor house*

Swaledale

The liveliness of Hawes gives way to the purposeful loneliness of Swaledale, which has not developed any sizeable market town along its main length until Richmond at its very end. On the descent from Askrigg Common, the remnants of lead mining are very evident at Oxnop Gill on the right of the road. The history of this cluster of houses is related in Hartley and Ingleby's *A Dales Heritage*. The upper part of the dale is also unusual in the strongly Nordic place names - Gunnerside, Thwaite and Muker demonstrating the origin of much of the hardness people associate with a northern, and in particular a Dales, accent.

The dale itself is on a greater scale than the other dales and is characterised less by quaintness than by the simple sense of space and power it evokes. Yet it is still full of natural history - much of Swaledale has been designated an Environmentally Sensitive Area, primarily to prevent the destruction of nature by over intensive farming. The most common sight in the dale is the local hardy Swaledale sheep. With its characteristically curly horns, it has been chosen as the emblem of the Yorkshire Dales National Park.

The story of the dale is dominated by lead mining, the whole valley being pockmarked with disused diggings and shafts.

Ivelet Bridge

Gunnerside, Low Row, Feetham

It takes no more than thirty seconds each to pass through these villages, yet they are perhaps the most unchanged and some of the most interesting villages on the route. Formerly mining villages, the population of the dale has shrunk to less than 20% of what it was in the heyday of lead mining, reflected in the quiet tranquillity of these villages. Gunnerside, in its name, is testament to the presence of Norse Vikings in this remote part of northern England, Gunner probably being the Norse chief who settled here, and side meaning pasture.

The ruins of the once highly productive Old Gang mines can be visited from Gunnerside. A way comes back down the valley by the Punch Bowl Inn in Feetham, and makes an interesting short walk.

Accommodation

Oxnop Hall
Gunnerside
01748 886253
Over £15

Rowleth End Guest House
Low Row
01748 886327
£16
SECURE/DRYING FACILITIES

Low Whita Farm Camping Barn
(near Scabba Wath Bridge)
Low Row
01748 884430
£3.75
SECURE FACILITIES

Hatter's Garth
Low Row
01748 886322

Punch Bowl Inn Bunkhouse
Low Row
01748 886233
B&B £13-£20
Bunkhouse £3-£5.50
BASIC WORKSHOP,
SECURE/DRYING FACILITIES

Camping

Low Whita Farm
Address as above
£2 per tent

Food and Drink

Punch Bowl Inn
Low Row
Bar meals £5-£10

Grinton

Grinton's most notable feature is its church, once known as the Cathedral of the Dales. Until 1580 Grinton was the only church in the dale, and bodies of the dead from the upper dale had to be carried down the valley by corpse bearers, who would stop at what is now the Punch Bowl at Feetham for refreshment. It was thought if the body did not follow the prescribed route, the soul would not reach heaven. The journey from the top of the dale could take several days.

At Grinton Smelt Mill

Accommodation

The Bridge Inn
Grinton
01748 884224
Over £15

The Smithy
Grinton
01748 884454
Up to £15

Grinton Youth Hostel
Grinton
01748 884206

Reeth

Although not on the Cycle Way, Reeth village is a very worthwhile diversion. The Swaledale Folk Museum is situated here, and has interesting displays on topics including lead mining, agriculture, religion, local dialect and local crafts. It is open 10.30 - 5.30, Easter - October 31st.

Intake Wood and Fremington Edge are natural features, a small way off the route, near Reeth, also showing the influence of Celtic man. Large Brigantian earthworks can be seen looking to the south from the wood: these are Venutius's defensive ramparts and were built entirely by human toil, without any mechanical aid.

LIVING HISTORY AT FREMINGTON EDGE

Pre Roman and Roman times

The impressive physical legacy of the Brigantines, northern Celts, can still be seen on the Dales Cycle Way, looking south from Intake Wood near Reeth in Swaledale. Large defensive ramparts can be identified here, built by the Brigantines to repel Roman advance in the first century AD.

The Brigantines originated around Lake Constance in Switzerland, and imported to the North their own pastoral lifestyle and Celtic social systems and beliefs. The 'high' or 'mighty' ones, as their name literally means, were initially a client state of the invading Romans. Following an internal split within the ruling family, Venutius overthrew his wife, and with his dominance came open hostility to the Roman presence.

However, the undoubted warlike ferocity of the Brigantines was no match for the steady conquest of the North, completed under the governership of Agricola from AD 79 onwards. The back-breaking labour resulting in the massive fortifications on Fremington Edge and at Stanwick in North Yorkshire demonstrate the seriousness with which the hill tribe treated the 'civilising and domesticating' threat posed by the invaders. They clearly valued their localised rural and pagan culture, as well as their own previously uncontested military dominance over the greater part of northern England.

Finally, the Brigantines were defeated by containment rather than outright military victory, evidenced by a ring of Roman forts on the flatter more easily settled land surrounding the Dales. Their leaders do not seem to have been Romanised in the southern style with the building of country villas and an embracing of urban sophistication and Roman culture. Similarly, the common people, probably little affected by the invaders' presence, seem to have withered into a vestigial Celtic culture, and finally perished with the more 'deep rooted' settlement of the Anglo-Saxons.

Had the Roman advance been successfully repelled, much of the North may possibly have enjoyed the direct legacy evidenced in the Gaelic tradition of Ireland and Scotland!

Head south out of Grinton, at once leaving the valley road to climb steeply to the foot of the moor. Take the right fork here and ascend to the panoramic surrounds of Grinton Moor. Descend, and immediately after passing a coniferous forest on the right, take a left (gated road) for Wensley and Preston-under-Scar.

Continue straight on this road for 4 kilometres into Wensley. In Wensley take the A684 for Hawes and cross over the river, then going left signposted for Carlton. Gradually climb on this road, looking back to see the villages of Wensley and Redmire, and a smoking quarry further up the hillside.

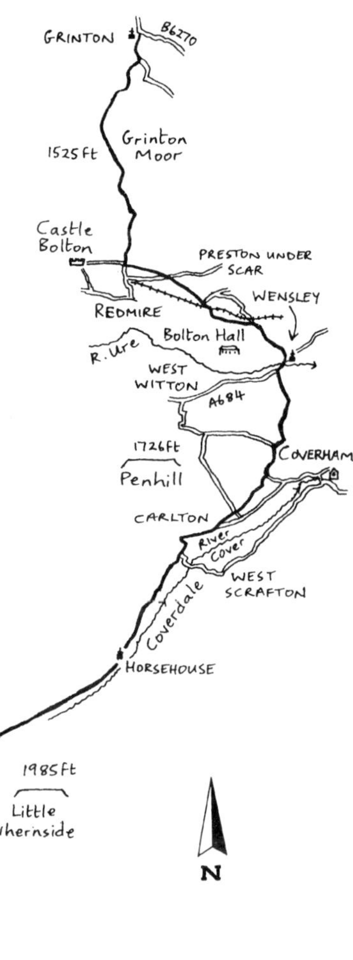

Take signposts for and passing through the small villages of Melmerby, Carlton, Horsehouse and the hamlet of Woodale. The minor road from Wensley over to Melmerby climbs quite steeply at some points, although there is no hint until you are in Horsehouse that you are beginning the serious ascent of a different dale.

Continue the ascent through Coverdale proper to reach the road summit at 1650ft above Park Rash. Commence a gradual, winding descent prior to a dangerous 20% drop coming into Kettlewell. Go right for the village centre.

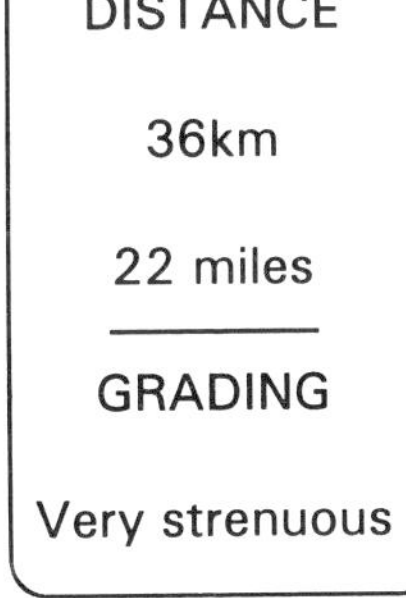

DISTANCE

36km

22 miles

GRADING

Very strenuous

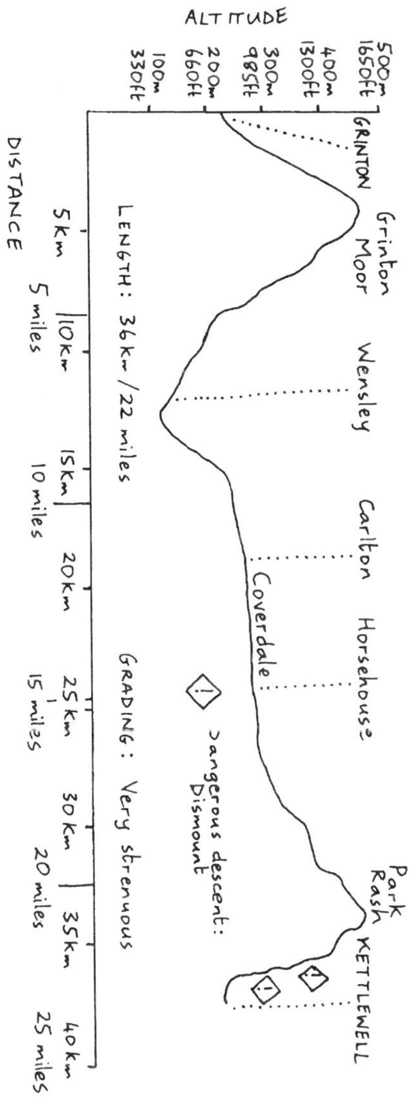

Bolton Castle

After the descent from Grinton Moor, instead of going left for Wensley, there is a right branch taking you straight to the castle. Built in the 14th century, this was the Scrope's northern stronghold (Lord Chancellor to Richard II). It cost the vast sum of twelve thousand pounds to build. It was one time residence of Mary, Queen of Scots, whilst rallying Catholic forces against the Elizabethan reformation. The castle, as displayed to visitors today, concentrates on the fact that Mary was held prisoner here in 1568 by the Scropes, as servants of Elizabeth I. Mary had fled from Scotland because of trouble caused by her own nobility, but in England proved the centre for plots against Elizabeth by northern Catholic nobility. She was eventually moved to Fotheringay and executed.

The castle is well preserved, and the interiors of many of the rooms have been restored. Mary's room in the south-west tower is complete with models of Mary and her advisors. The ground floor courtyard and surrounding rooms show how the lower and outer rooms were virtually a village within the castle. Here was produced all that was needed for the inhabitants to live independently of the outside world, including a mill, kitchens and a blacksmith. The castle eventually fell into disuse after the Civil War. Like Middleham, several people made cottage homes in the derelict ruins.

Open: March-November 10am-5pm: For winter opening, ring 01969 23981

Adults £2.50
Children £1.50

Bolton Castle

Wensley

The contrast between Wensley and its northerly neighbours in Swaledale is quite marked. In contrast to the air of sober hardiness of places such as Low Row, Wensley has a well kept affluence about it. Its quaintness is that of a southern village, although architecturally it is still recognisably a Dales village.

On the Leyburn road exiting the village, a stone memorial cross recites the names of those villagers who served in the World Wars, and also those who died. It is a reminder of the far reaching effects of the conflict that they should reach into the nooks and corners of rural England, and affect the daily lives of all who lived there. Listed on the memorial are the Orde Powletts, previous owners of Bolton Castle and representatives of the constituency in Parliament.

Other features of the village are the stone water pump in the central square, and the church. The latter displays the coats of arms of friends of the Scropes, the medieval family that dominated the area and inhabited Bolton Castle. In the church-yard there are still the remains of the original market cross, demonstrating the fact that Wensley was once an important market town. The economic life of the town was decimated in the mid sixteenth century, which turned it temporarily into a ghost town. Leyburn, being less severely effected, overtook it as a market town, and in many ways it seems the vitality of the place hasn't recovered.

The stately gates on one side of the centre mark the entrance to Bolton Hall, home originally to the Powlett family who married into the Scropes and succeeded them as the local patrons. A footpath cuts through the hall's grounds back towards Preston-under-Scar, and passes close to 'Nanny Doune's well and tree'. Local folklore says this was the local postlady who slept in the tree, and who, in the usual folklore tradition, haunts the tree!

Food and drink

The Three Horseshoes
Wensley
Beers: Theakstons, Tetleys,
Websters, John Smiths

Camping

Swan Farm
Redmire

Coverham Abbey and Middleham Castle

Ruins of this once rich Cistercian abbey can be visited by a short detour from the route at Agglethorpe, in the bottom of Coverdale. The trip can also be extended to Middleham, home of the castle which was the power base for Richard III's usurpation of the monarchy. It was also the centre of the forest of Wensleydale, when much of the valley was a royal forest used for hunting. The abbey is today mainly weathered ruins, blended eclectically with surrounding countryside and farm buildings. Unlike Bolton Abbey, the fabric of the building was largely destroyed at the Dissolution.

The gatehouse,
Coverham Abbey

Jervaulx Abbey

A further detour, 4½ miles north-west of Masham. The abbey declined to its present minimal remains after the last abbot was hanged in 1537, during Henry's Reformation. Like Coverham, it is the delicate setting which make the scene, rather than the ruins themselves.

Horsehouse

Coverdale

Coverdale seems abandoned to the wild, although enclosures still show the presence of man: there are precious few settlements in its upper reaches, and the road dips and twists over the deeply etched gills carving out its side. Along with the road that leads up Kingsdale, the road that winds to the top of Coverdale is the quietest on the Cycle Way. In its day, however, it was on the main coaching route from London to Richmond, but now sees only a few locals and tourists. Indeed, Horsehouse is so called because the coach's horses are said to have been stabled here overnight on the route. The same village also housed travellers and drovers from Scotland. Again, as in the case of Askrigg, local accounts record murders of these comparatively rich Scottish traders. Horsehouse is the last real village before the climb into the wilds of Coverdale.

It was from here that Miles Coverdale, translator of the new bible of 1526, took his name. The dale's other main claim to fame is that, at its northern end, it shares in the horse training industry for which Middleham is so renowned.

Accommodation

Coverlea
Carlton in Coverdale
01969 40248
£13
SECURE/DRYING FACILITIES

Foresters Arms
Carlton in Coverdale
01969 40272
£27.50

Thwaite Arms, Horsehouse
01969 40206   £16.50
POSSIBLE DRYING/LAUNDRY FACILITIES BY ARRANGEMENT

Camping

Enquire at the Thwaite Arms
£2 per person

Manor Farm
Horsehouse

Food and Drink

Thwaite Arms, Horsehouse
Bar meals generally under £5
Beers: Theakstons

LIVING HISTORY AT MIDDLEHAM AND COVERDALE

Medieval times: waxing and waning of the Northern power base

The newly found role of the Dales as part of a Northern buffer zone, where nobles enjoyed the freedoms of what were their own mini-kingdoms, posed threats to the central power throughout the centuries.

In 1215 several northern nobles participated in the rising that led to Magna Carta, but it was essentially the blood feud prosaically named the Wars of the Roses that saw the North as the crucial area for the nation's future, as rival descendants of the monarch fought each other for the privileges of becoming the ruling house of the country. Yorkists emerged victorious and Middleham Castle in Wensleydale is a worthwhile diversion. It was home to Richard III, and arguably the greatest noble the country has ever seen, Warwick the kingmaker.

The Tudor monarchy, with its regulating and centralizing power, much curtailed the independent power of the so-called Council of the North. Its lords' franchises and liberties were reduced, and in 1603 many of the major aristocrats raison d'être was removed with the Union of the English and Scottish crowns. This process saw savage regional counter-action in the form of the 16th century Pilgrimage of Grace and a rising of Catholic gentry.

The former was a reaction against the despoilation and threat to the social structure posed by Henry VIII's rape of Northern monastic wealth, whose treasures were diverted to his own coffers. It was also a protest against the inflation which was causing much of the North to sink into poverty and backwardness, a trend which continued until after the Civil War. The pilgrimage's founder, Robert Aske, came from the Dales, and the movement occupied the important strongholds of Coverham Abbey and Middleham Castle.

The Civil War saw the eclipse of the north, which had little role to play for the mercantilist, Puritanical, southern based classes who were the main supporters of the Parliamentarians. The loss of its military function and its back seat role in the Civil War power struggle condemned the north to such a position until the late 1700's.

The 17th century did, however, see Puritan preachers making inroads in the more inaccessible northern areas of the Dales, now that the unchallenged control of Rome over the minds of Englishmen had been shattered. Fox's and Wesley's tours of the area must have presented a similar spectacle to present day born-again preachers, with their preachings of individual enlightenment through the acceptance of Quakerism and Methodism respectively.

Kettlewell

Kettlewell attracts much of the tourist trade passing north on the B6160 up the valley, and can be excessively busy at peak times such as summer weekends or bank holidays. However, it still has a great deal of charm, being centred on a tiny beck running through its middle and claiming three public houses. The 'modern' church has a 12th century tub font, and windows to commemorate men who died in World War Two.

Accommodation

The Elms
Middle Lane
01756 760224
£15-£20

Cam Lodge
01756 760276
£15-£20

Youth Hostel
Whernside House
01756 760232

Cycle shop

W. Wilkinson
The Garage

A corner of Kettlewell

From the village centre bridge by the Racehorses and the Bluebell hotels, don't head for the Wharfe bridge on the main road down-dale, but go left to a junction under a maypole, just before the church and the Kings Head pub. Here turn right. This parallel back road heads down the east side of the dale, with the Wharfe on your right. Continue through Conistone, passing through Grass Wood and sweeping left into Grassington. There are superb views of the west bank of Wharfedale on this stretch, in particular the highly distinctive cliff facade of Kilnsey Crag, a favourite 'playground' for devotees of severe limestone climbs.

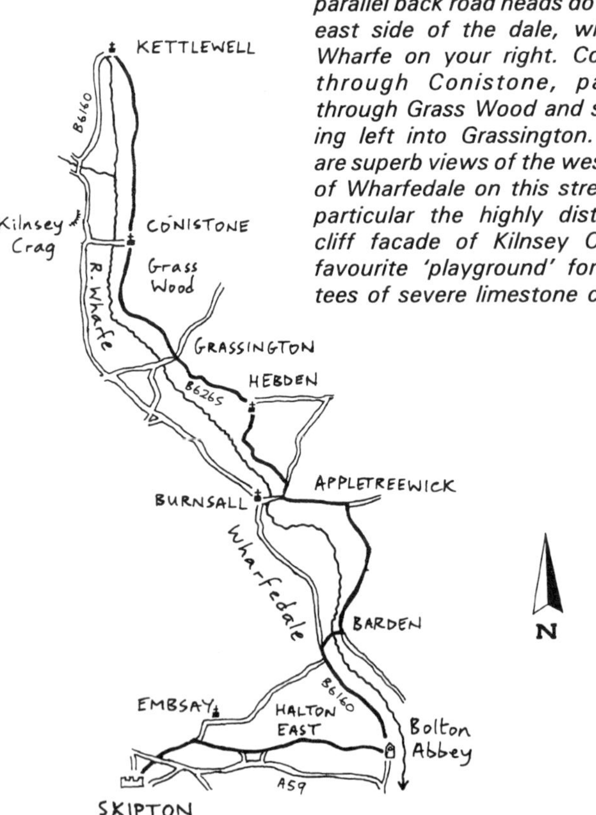

Go past Grassington town centre on your left on the B6265 to Hebden. In Hebden turn right just past the pub. There are lofty vistas over Burnsall as you wend your way down the east bank of the Wharfe. Turn right at the T-junction and then left at the next one to take you into Appletreewick. Retrace your outward steps with a right turn after Appletreewick, then fork right over Barden Bridge and go left towards Bolton Abbey on the B6160.

Follow the river to Bolton Abbey, passing above the Strid, and past the Cavendish memorial fountain. Turn first right in the village. Good views over the narrow, craggy, wooded river can be glimpsed on this stretch. Continue through Halton East, and then left on reaching Embsay to return to Skipton.

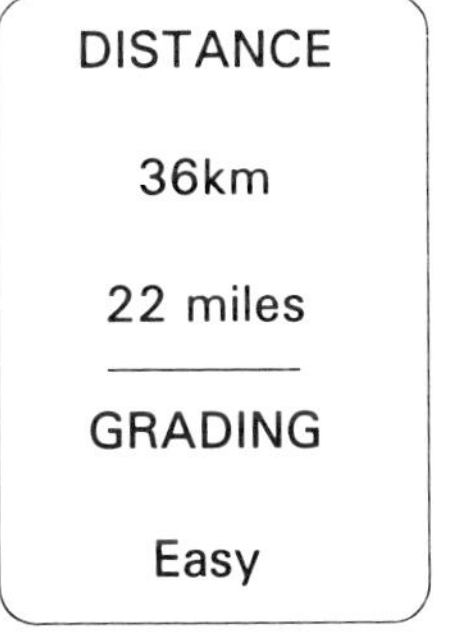

DISTANCE

36km

22 miles

GRADING

Easy

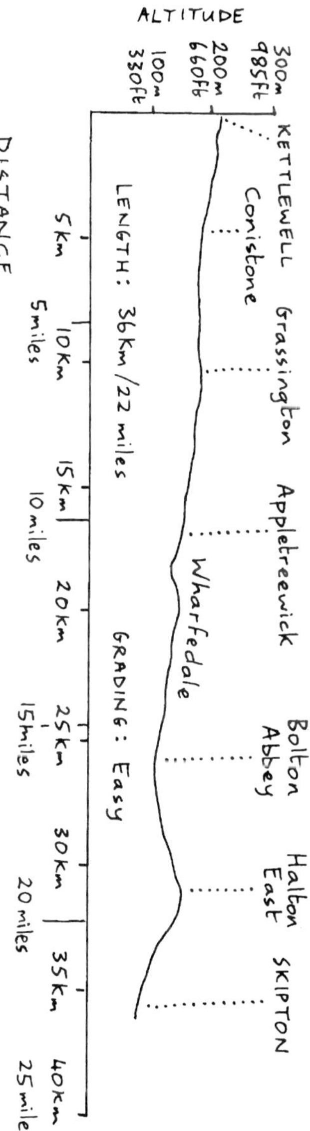

Kilnsey Crag

*St. Mary's,
Conistone*

Grassington

Grassington today centres physically and economically around the long rising main street and the cobbled market square at its southern end. The Upper Wharfedale Folk Museum is on the cobbled square (open daily 2.00 - 4.30pm, entrance 40p). The road climbing through the square continues out of the village, offering superb views of surrounding countryside and leads to extensive disused lead mines that are well worth a visit. These mines, together with textiles, were the source of most of the town's wealth. In the eighteenth and nineteenth centuries the

66

lead mines above Grassington comprised one of the most complex systems of waterwheels, artificial watercourses and grinding and smelting mills in the whole of Europe.

Cupola flue and chimney at the lead mines, Grassington Moor

Accommodation

Town Head Guest House
01756 752811
£13 and above

Chapel Fold Guest House
01756 752075

Brownfold Cottage (off Main Street)
01756 752314
£13-£16
SECURE/DRYING FACILITIES

Food and drink

Cobblestones Cafe
The Square
Snacks under £5

Grassington House Hotel
The Square
£5 and above

Black Horse Hotel
Garrs Lane
£5 and above
Beers: Free House -
Black Sheep,Tetleys,Theakstons

Devonshire Arms
The Square
Bar meals £5
Beers: Theakstons

Paul and Cheryl's
Main Street
High class cuisine
Meals generally over £5

There is a fish and chip shop
on Garrs Lane

Mountain bike hire

The Mountaineer and Rambler, Pletts Barn   01756 75226

THE JAKEY - local slang for this short-cut between the Square and Wood Lane car park

THE WOGGINS - Further colourful local dialect for this charming, partly covered alleyway

LADY WELL - by the bridge. One of the ancient holy wells of Craven. Situated near Ladywell Cottage, formerly a medieval crook house.

PLETT'S BARN - Now adapted for commercial purposes, this building has retained some original features such as the dovecotes

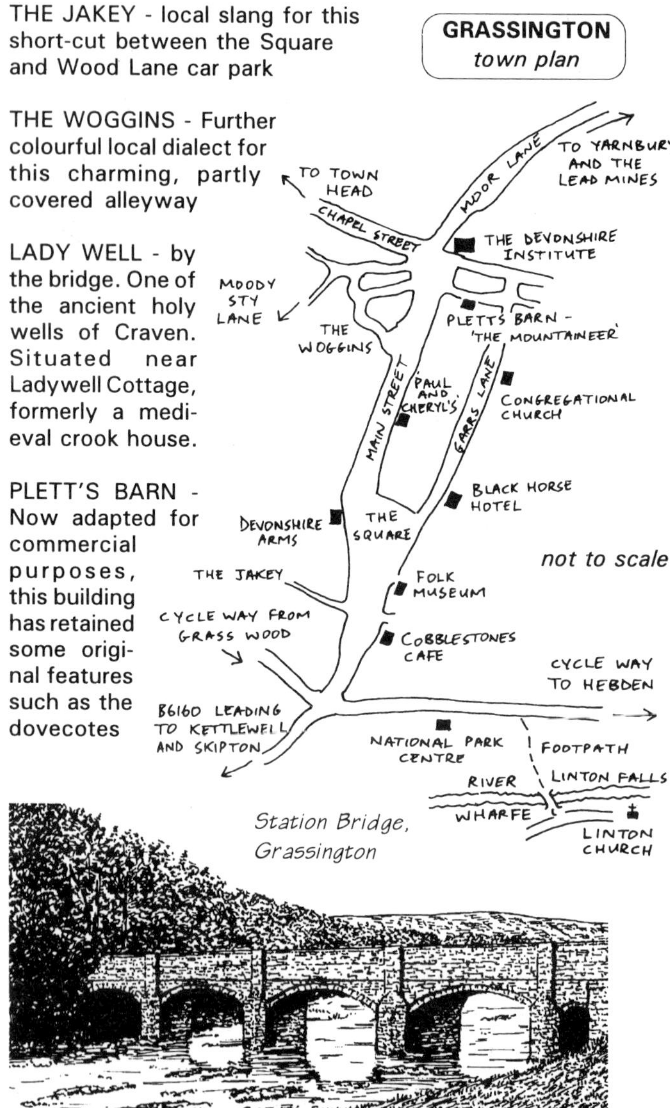

Station Bridge, Grassington

Linton

The short walk to nearby Linton church past Linton Falls is well worth the effort. Linton church is a truly beautiful example of medieval architecture. One of the roof bosses shows the 'Green Man', an ancient fertility symbol reminding you the church is built on a previously pagan ritual site, and reflects the way local traditions blended with local christianity.

Accommodation

Linton Youth Hostel
The Old Rectory
01756 752400

At Linton Falls
(the old bridge now has
a wooden replacement)

Hebden

Accommodation/food and drink

Clarendon Hotel
01756 752446
£15-£20
Snacks less than £5 and full meals £5-£10
Beers: Tetleys/free house

Bolton Abbey

Privately owned by the Duke and Duchess of Devonshire, the priory ruins are set amid a backdrop of spectacular sylvan beauty, comprising ancient oak and ash trees. The site may be too developed for some tastes, especially after the building of a new, out of character 'licensed cafe' by the riverside car park. A £2 motorists' entrance fee gives access to over thirty miles of footpaths as well as the priory ruins.

The Hole in the Wall, Bolton Abbey

Bolton Priory

Halton East

The Old Hall, Halton East

Set in this farming hamlet is the 17th century Old Hall, now divided into two dwellings. Visible to the public are the two most interesting faces, namely the east and south fronts. These display the same attractive facade, including mullioned and transomed windows.

*Tithe Barn,
Bolton Abbey*

LIVING HISTORY AT BOLTON ABBEY

The Norman religious revival

Following the death and destruction caused largely by William the Conqueror's crushing of northern rebellions, a monastic revival took place. In 1155 Augustinians moved from Embsay to found a priory on the present site of Bolton Abbey. It was one of 180 Augustinian houses in England.

The creed of Augustinians was based on 'The Rule' - the central writings of St Augustine of Hippo, as further amended by Papal intervention. The daily lives of the 'Black Canons' were supposedly based around the vows of chastity, poverty and obedience that they took on entering the order. Their lives were to be devoted to the worship of God with as little concern as possible for worldly distractions. This lifestyle contrasts strongly to the manual self sufficiency of the 'White Monks' or Cistercian order apparent at Fountains Abbey. According to the archives of the estate owners, it seems some of the canons found their esoteric lifestyle, and a routine that included at least six services every day, rather demanding. Sufficient, in fact, for them to seek secular temptations by sneaking out of the priory when the main gates were opened to allow visitors in.

The priory was, despite its other wordly aspirations, only able to function by having a powerful local patron (the Clifford family after 1310), and itself exploiting its position as a powerful local landowner. The majority of the income that allowed the canons the luxury of their solitude and contemplation came from wool, corn, livestock sales, and tithes extracted from land granted to the priory by the nobility.

The Dissolution prompted by Henry VIII's anti papal rage shattered this state of affairs forever in 1539, when the prior of the abbey was forced to surrender the buildings to the King's commissioners. The redistribution of the wealth of Bolton Priory to the King and his favourites was a supreme example of ruthless asset stripping, which make the present day dismantling of manufacturing industry in the north seem comparativly genteel. At its height, the priory employed 200 of the locals as craftsmen, foresters and shepherds, amongst other things. Lead was stripped from the roof, silver went to the king's treasury, canons were pensioned off and the greater part of the estate was bought by Henry Clifford, the local Earl.

The central buildings became absorbed within the new Church of England and many of the canons, chameleon-like, changed the hue of their beliefs, although the North was to retain strong papal sympathies. Some of the old buildings were turned into houses or rented to local businesses.

The church as it now was, was lucky in the paternalistic attitude of many of its lordly patrons over the coming centuries. In the mid 17th century Lady Anne Clifford inherited the estates that had previously unjustly been denied her by her male predecessors, and renovated the priory that had been allowed to fall into some disrepair. Similarly, from 1867-1917 a further programme of beautification was undertaken by the 6th and 7th Dukes of Devonshire, both great patrons of the arts.

Full details of these changes can be found in a publication at Bolton Abbey (Bolton Abbey and its Church - Peter Watkins: a very detailed history of the priory, church and its estates).

Gatehouse, Skipton Castle

RECORD OF THE JOURNEY

Date	Place		Kilometres		Times		Comments
			daily	total	arrive	depart	
	Skipton		-	-			
	Embsay		3	3			
	Barden Tower		12	12			
	Burnsall		16	16			
	Hetton	STAGE 1	25	25			
	Airton		31	31			
	Malham		36	36			
	Malham Tarn		5	41			
	Stainforth		14	50			
	Settle	STAGE 2	18	54			
	Eldroth		24˙	60			
	Clapham		32	68			
	Ingleton		38	74			
	White Shaw Moss		11	85			
	Dent		17	91			
	Cowgill	STAGE 3	24	98			
	Newby Head		29	103			
	Hawes		39	113			

Date	Place	Kilometres		Times		Comments
		daily	total	arrive	depart	
	Askrigg	8	121			
	Askrigg Common	13	126			
	Gunnerside	19	132			
	Low Row STAGE 4	24	137			
	Grinton	30	143			
	Grinton Moor	4	147			
	Preston under Scar	10	153			
	Wensley	12	155			
	Carlton STAGE 5	19	162			
	Horsehouse	25	168			
	Park Rash road top	33	176			
	Kettlewell	36	179			
	Conistone	5	184			
	Grassington STAGE 6	11	190			
	Hebden	14	193			
	Appletreewick	17	196			
	Bolton Abbey	26	205			
	Skipton	36	215			

THE MOUNTAIN BIKE CODE OF CONDUCT

RIGHTS OF WAY

* *Bridleways* - open to cyclists, but you must give way to walkers and horse riders

* *Byways* - Usually unsurfaced tracks open to cyclists. As well as walkers and cyclists, you may meet occasional vehicles which also have a right of access.

* *Public footpaths* - no right to cycle exists

Look out for posts from the highway, or waymarking arrows (blue for bridleways, red for byways and yellow for footpaths)

NB The above rights do not apply in Scotland

OTHER ACCESS

* *Open land* - on most upland, moorland and farmland, cyclists normally have no right of access without express permission of the landowner.

* *Towpaths* - a British Waterways cycling permit is required for cyclists wishing to use their canal towpaths.

* *Pavements* - cycling is not permitted on pavements

* *Designated cycle paths* - look out for designated cycle paths or bicycle routes which may be found in urban areas, on Forestry Commission land, disused railway lines or other open spaces.

OTHER INFORMATION

* Cyclists must adhere to the Highway Code. A detailed map is recommended for more adventurous trips.

FOLLOW THE COUNTRY CODE

* Enjoy the countryside and respect its life and work
* Guard against all risk of fire
* Fasten all gates
* Keep dogs under close control
* Keep to rights of way across farmland
* Use gates and stiles to cross fences, hedges and walls
* Leave livestock, crops and machinery alone
* Take your litter home
* Help to keep all water clean
* Protect wildlife, plants and trees
* Take special care of country roads
* Make no unnecessary noise

SAFETY

* Ensure that your bike is safe to ride and prepared for all
  emergencies
* You are required by law to display working lights after dark
  (front and rear)
* Always carry some form of identification
* Always tell someone where you are going
* Learn to apply the basic principles of first aid
* Reflective materials on your clothes or bike can save your life
* For safety on Mountains refer to the British Mountaineering
  Council publication *Safety on Mountains*
* Ride under control when going downhill, since this is often
  when serious accidents occur
* If you intend to ride fast off-road it is advisable to wear a
  helmet
* Particular care should be taken on unstable or wet surfaces

COMPETITIONS

* Events are organised by a number of clubs and national bodies.
  They can only take place with the permission of the landowner
  and/or highway authorities as appropriate.

HILLSIDE GUIDES

■ *Circular Walks - Yorkshire Dales*

WHARFEDALE
THREE PEAKS
WENSLEYDALE
SWALEDALE
HOWGILL FELLS
NIDDERDALE
MALHAMDALE

■ *Circular Walks - North York Moors*

WESTERN MOORS
SOUTHERN MOORS
NORTHERN MOORS

■ *Circular Walks - South Pennines*

BRONTE COUNTRY
CALDERDALE
ILKLEY MOOR

■ *Circular Walks - Lancashire*

BOWLAND
PENDLE & the RIBBLE

■ *Circular Walks - North Pennines*

TEESDALE
EDEN VALLEY

■ *Circular Walks - Peak District*

NORTHERN PEAK
CENTRAL PEAK

■ **WALKING COUNTRY TRIVIA QUIZ** ■
Over 1000 questions on the great outdoors

ACROSS THE NORTH

■ *Long Distance Walks*

THE COAST TO COAST WALK
DALES WAY COMPANION
CLEVELAND WAY COMPANION
FURNESS WAY
WESTMORLAND WAY
CUMBERLAND WAY
NORTH BOWLAND TRAVERSE (David Johnson)
LADY ANNE'S WAY (Sheila Gordon)

■ *Hillwalking - Lake District*

OVER LAKELAND MOUNTAINS - the 2000ft peaks
OVER LAKELAND FELLS - the sub-2000ft fells

■ *Yorkshire Pub Walks* by Valerie Yewdall

HARROGATE & the WHARFE VALLEY
HAWORTH & the AIRE VALLEY

■ *BIKING COUNTRY* by Richard Peace

YORKSHIRE DALES CYCLE WAY
WEST YORKSHIRE CYCLE WAY
MOUNTAIN BIKING - WEST & SOUTH YORKSHIRE
GLASGOW Clyde Valley & Loch Lomond

■ *POCKET BIKING GUIDES* by Paul Hannon

AIRE VALLEY   **CALDERDALE**

■ *Large format colour hardback* ■

FREEDOM OF THE DALES
Exploring the Yorkshire Dales on Foot

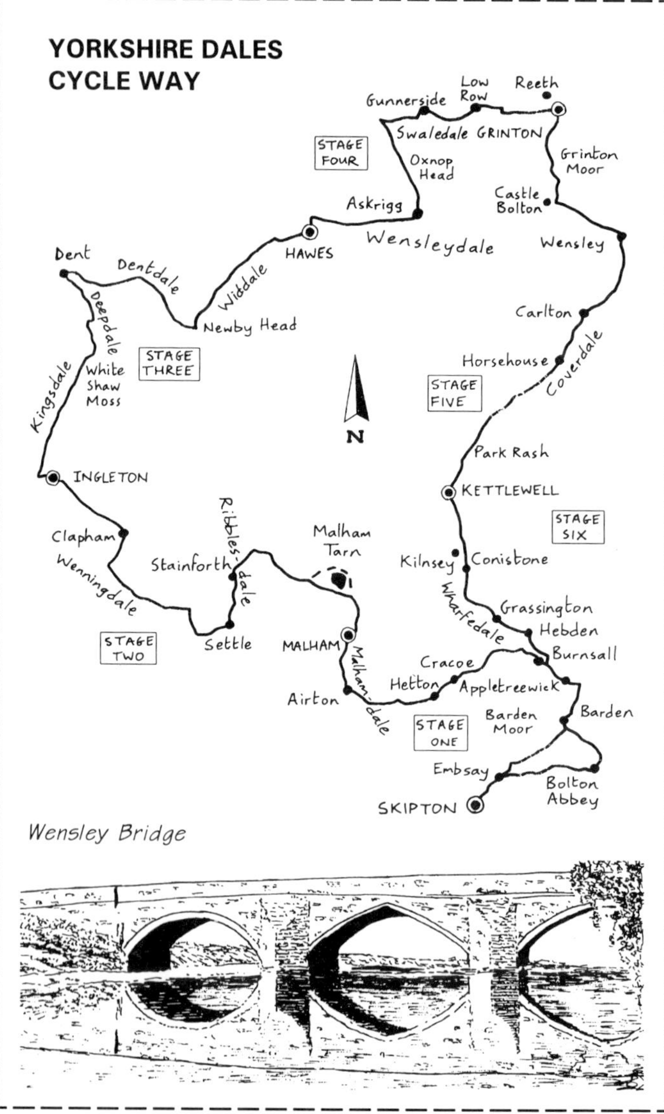

Wensley Bridge